Thinking as Researchers Innovative Research Methodology Content and Methods

Thinking as Researchers Innovative Research Methodology Content and Methods

Nagwa Babiker Abdulla Yousif

&

Shadia Abdelrahim Mohammed Daoud

To order additional copies of this book, contact:
Xlibris
844-714-8691
www.Xlibris.com
Orders@Xlibris.com
842444

Ajman University
and
Ahfad University for Women

Thinking as Researchers
Innovative Research Methodology
Content and Methods

Shadia Abdelrahim Mohammed Daoud[1]
Nagwa Babiker Abdulla Yousif[2,3]

November 1, 2022

1   Ahfad University for Women, School of Rural Extension Education and Development, Sudan

2   College of Humanities and Sciences, Ajman University, Ajman, UAE

3   Humanities and Social Sciences Research Center (HSSRC), Ajman University, Ajman, UAE

CONTENTS

Section 1 : Critical Thinking and Innovative Teaching of Research Methods (Instructors)

Section 2 : Syllabus of Research
Methods for the Students

PREFACE

Research is crucial in an academic's promotion and knowledge-building. But its understanding and the practices of research are dilemma and challenges in the academic domain. Literatures indicated the research methods is not the most enjoyable course for the students to take nor the most enjoyable course for the teachers to teach. It is, nevertheless, one of the most important courses in the educational curriculum. The current structure and content of many research methods courses cannot adequately support students to acquire the competencies they need to deal with complex data and new analytical tools. What is more, those involved in the teaching of research methods courses tend to teach the same content for many years, in the same way, despite the changing nature of data, for instance, big data and analytics, and the complexity of the environment. University teachers often teach the subject based on their individual expertise gained through graduate training or professional experience. However, the majority of the teachers of the research methods did not acquire formal degrees in the field; some are self-taught, while others acquired the knowledge of the subject either through practice or courses they took during postgraduate education. Incorporating research in the undergraduate curriculum allows students to gain the knowledge and skills to learn the research process, not to conduct it, per se, but rather use research to bridge the gap between knowledge and critical decision-making.

This book considers the research process as not simply collecting data, evidence, or "facts," then piecing together this preexisting information into a paper. Instead, the research process is about inquiry—asking questions and developing answers through serious critical thinking and thoughtful reflection.

Why do students face difficulty in understanding researches? The students' lack of critical thinking and creativity is widely recognized as the main cause, considering critical thinking is a core competency and a precursor to research. The importance of critical-thinking skills in research is, therefore, huge; without which, researchers may even lack the confidence to challenge their assumptions (Facione, P. A., 2000; Lawson, T. J., 1995).

Teaching should make thinking visible. This concerns the thinking of the teachers and the students. The teacher should model scientific thinking to help students understand how problems are solved, for example, by means of simulations and visualizations (Perrone, L. F., 2014).

The students should be prompted to report on their ideas, critique and analyze their progress, and reflect on the nature of science (Bambrick-Santoyo, P., 2010). Creativity in research provides concrete guidance on developing creativity for anyone doing or mentoring research. By focusing attention on how research happens as well as its outputs, you can increase your ability to address research challenges and produce the outputs you care about (Halpern, D. F., 2001).

Why is creativity important in research? Motivated by curiosity on top of a vast knowledge base, creativity allows one to shake up the normal way of thinking and come up with new solutions to a problem. Innovation, on the other hand, is creating something new that has obvious value to others (Silvia, P. J., 2012).

By practicing critical thinking, students are allowing themselves not only to solve problems, but also come up with new and creative ideas to do so. Critical thinking allows us to analyze these ideas and adjust them accordingly. Critical-thinking skills are necessary for students preparing for and/or enrolled in professional programs, especially the ability to evaluate and synthesize information, which are vital for problem-solving. Essentially, critical thinking is learning to think independently and to develop one's opinions supported by existing evidence. In learning scenarios that promote and foster problem-solving and critical-thinking skills, it is much more difficult for the student to simply adhere to the role of the passive student; rather, this type of learning prompts the student to assume the role of a self-reliant thinker and researcher. Critical thinking is important for the students. It helps them to think creatively, and it keeps them from becoming narrow (Gellin, A., 2003).

Researcher Jane Qinjuan Zhang (2009) writes that critical thinking enables students to assess their learning styles, strengths, and weaknesses and allows them to take ownership of their education.

How does research develop critical thinking? Academic research focuses on the creation of new ideas, perspectives, and arguments. The researcher seeks relevant information in articles, books, and other sources then develops an informed point of view within this ongoing "conversation" among researchers (Ku, K. Y., 2009).

This book is based on the experiences of the authors working on teaching and supervising of research at undergraduate and graduate levels, particularly informing the authors of the challenges facing the students to think as the researchers. Think as researchers is a collective role of the students and the instructors of research methodology. The book aims to critically analyze the concepts of critical thinking and creativity and their role and use in research to motivate students to think as researchers, to explore the innovative contents and methods of teaching the research methods that promote to students to think as researchers.

The book is organized into two sections. Section 1 has two chapters and is for the instructors, while Section 2 has one chapter and is for the students. Chapter 1 of Section 1 presents the effective role of critical thinking and creativity on research. Chapter 2 explores innovative methods of teaching research that promotes thinking as researchers to students. A syllabus of research methods that promotes to students to think as researchers is provided in Chapter 3.

SECTION 1

CHAPTER 1

Critical Thinking

1.1. Background

Critical thinking is widely recognized as a core competency and a precursor to research. Critical-thinking skills are necessary for students preparing for and/or enrolled in professional programs, especially the ability to evaluate and synthesize information, which are vital for problem-solving. Deficiencies in critical-thinking skills among students may rest with the educational system itself, which often stresses memorization of voluminous amounts of material essentially unrelated to any type of application at all. Essentially, critical thinking is learning to think independently and to develop one's opinions supported by existing evidence (Fischer, S. C.; Spiker, V. A.; and Riedel, S. L., 2009; Facione, P. A., 2000).

In learning scenarios that promote and foster problem-solving and critical-thinking skills, it is much more difficult for the student to simply adhere to the role of the passive student; rather, this type of learning prompts the student to assume the role of a self-reliant thinker and researcher. Attaining critical-thinking skills does not come without its challenges as students must be able to manage a vast array of resources within a series of complex network systems (Dingfelder, S. F., 2005; Newell, K. M., Kinesiology, 2007).

This is especially true when students are asked to write research paper, which is one of the most common methods for teaching critical-thinking skills (De Sanchez, M. A., 1995).

1.2. Some Points

Arguably, an important component of critical-thinking skills is the ability to critically examine and understand published research in one's professional area of interest. Requiring students to critique published research is one way of addressing the goal of teaching students to critically evaluate research while gaining experience doing it. At its very essence, scientific research is a problem-based learning activity that sharpens critical-thinking skills (Dingfelder, S. F., 2005).

The question then arises as to the extent which critical thinking is initiated during a student's education in any given institution in higher education. As such, any focus on learning without critical thought becomes less meaningful, thereby disengaging students from any formal training and experience, specifically as it relates to critically reviewing and evaluating research (Lawson, T. J., 1999; Yanchar, S.C.; Slife, B. D., 2004).

An even greater challenge, and one that provides a framework for differentiating between different levels of learning and thought by incorporating reasoning and critical-thinking skills to a greater degree, is to actually engage students in the scientific method (Zablotsky, D., 2001).

Students actively participate in the formulation of a research question, data collection, and statistical analysis as a means of creating a learning environment that encourages or even forces them to engage in critical thinking and higher level reasoning (Gellin, A., 2003).

1.3. Why is it important to use critical thinking in research?

Critical thinking is important in life. It helps students think creatively—outside the box. It keeps you from becoming narrow. Researcher Jane Qinjuan Zhang (2009) writes that critical thinking enables students to assess their learning styles, strengths, and weaknesses and allows them to take ownership of their education.

1.4. How does research develop critical thinking?

Academic research focuses on the creation of new ideas, perspectives, and arguments. The researcher seeks relevant information in articles, books, and other sources then develops an informed point of view within this ongoing "conversation" among researchers (Dre, P.; Chatwin, J.; Collins, S., 2001).

1.5. Critical-Thinking Methodology

Critical thinking is the intellectually disciplined process of actively and skillfully conceptualizing, applying, analyzing, synthesizing, and/or evaluating information gathered from or generated by observation, experience, reflection, reasoning, or communication as a guide to belief and action (Ku, K. Y., 2009).

1.6. Critical-Thinking Skills Examples

- Analytical thinking
- Good communication
- Creative thinking
- Open-mindedness
- Ability to solve problems
- Asking thoughtful questions
- Promoting a teamwork approach to problem-solving
1. Self-evaluating your contributions to company goals (McPeck, J. E., 1990; O'Hare, L. O., and McGuinness, C., 2009)

1.7. Steps of Critical Thinking

- Identify the problem or question
- Gather data, opinions, and arguments
- Analyze and evaluate the data
- Identify assumptions
- Establish significance
- Make a decision/reach a conclusion
- Present or communicate (Lamm, A. J., 2015; Facione, P., 2007)

1.8. Good Critical Thinkers

Good critical thinkers are able to stay as objective as possible when looking at information or a situation. They focus on facts and on the scientific evaluation of the information at hand. Objective thinkers seek to keep their emotions and those of others from affecting their judgment (Gellin, A., 2003).

1.9. Are we born with critical-thinking skills?

Children are not born with the power to think critically, nor do they develop this ability naturally beyond survival-level thinking. Critical thinking is a learned ability that must be taught. Most individuals never learn it. Critical thinking cannot be taught reliably to students by peers or by most parents (Thayer-Bacon, B. J., 2000).

1.10. Can you teach critical thinking?

Decades of cognitive research point to a disappointing answer: not really. People who have sought to teach critical thinking have assumed it is a skill, like riding a bicycle, and that like other skills, once you learn it, you can apply it in any situation (Halpern, D. F., 2001; Pithers, R. T., and Soden, R., 2000).

1.11. Exercises

Six Thinking Hats

Edward de Bono
Dr. Edward de Bono (2005) used his expertise to promote more effective creative thinking and decision-making. The Six Thinking Hats is one such technique.

The main idea is to have the group only "wear one hat at a time" when considering a problem. The wearing of the hat is metaphorical. At any one time, everyone will wear the same color, in other words, look at the problem at hand from only one perspective, the perspective indicated by the hat color.

White Hat Thinking: Just the Facts

The white hat calls for information known or needed. "The facts, just the facts." When you ask for white hat, think you are asking what information is needed, what is available, and how it can be obtained.

Yellow Hat Thinking: Benefits, Pluses

The yellow hat explores the positives and probes for value and benefit. The yellow hat role is for discussing *only* the positive view of problems and solution possibilities. We are often better with the black hat. We are good at seeing what won't work as opposed to what will.

Black Hat Thinking: Difficulties, Problems

The black hat is judgment—the devil's advocate or why something may not work. Spots the difficulties and dangers. Probably the most powerful and useful of the hats but a problem if overused. When you think of black, think of negative or caution. The black hat is for critical judgment. It points out what cannot be done. The hope is that the black hat role will prevent us from making mistakes.

Red Hat Thinking: Feelings, Gut Instinct, Intuition

The red hat signifies feelings, hunches, and intuition. When using this hat, you can express emotions and feelings and share fears, likes, dislikes, loves, and hates. People don't need to justify their statements. The red hat allows feelings to be expressed. Once they are stated, people can move on to a more constructive approach.

It is not the logical part of thinking that changes emotions but the perceptual part. If we see something differently, our emotions may alter with the altered perception.

Edward de Bono

Green Hat Thinking: Creativity, Ideas, Possibilities

The green hat is an opportunity to express new concepts and new perceptions. Could this be done in another way? Might there be another explanation? Does anyone have another idea?

Blue Hat Thinking: Managing the Thinking

It's the control mechanism that ensures the Six Thinking Hats guidelines are observed. The blue hat is the hardest one to understand. It deals with controlling the thinking process. The blue hat is often "given" to one person who controls what hat will be "worn," hence controlling the type of thinking being used. The blue hat comments on the thinking being used, asks for conclusions, decisions, etc. The blue hat can move from person to person or can be a chairperson (De Bono, E., 2005)

CHAPTER 2

Innovative Teaching Methods of Research Methods

2.1. Background and Some Points

Some authors wrote on research methodology to reflect the creativity and critical thinking of the students (S., Handfield, T. & Restall, G. (2009), Willingham, D. T. (2007), Tim van Gelder (2005), Barraket, J. (2005), Campisi, J. & Finn, K. E. (2011), Earley, M. A. (2014), Froyd, J. E. (2007). Kilburn, D., Nind, M. & Wiles, R. (2014), Lewthwaite, S. & Nind, M. (2016) & Bailey, (1997).

A research methodology course needs to be redesigned to reflect the creativity and critical thinking of the students. The instructors change to use innovative methods of teaching. There are many academics who believe that research methodology is difficult to teach. The tried-and-tested classroom-based approaches used in most other subjects do not sufficiently address the nuances students need to be aware of to understand the implications of research techniques adequately to become a successful academic researcher. This is because, ultimately, research methodology needs to be about more than simply collecting data and then manipulating it. Teachers of research methods find it challenging to teach research methods because courses on research methods often bring together students from a wide range of disciplines, with different prior knowledge, diverse interests and expectations. Also, teachers of research methods face additional problems because the content of a research methodology course is highly multidisciplinary and too demanding to be effectively managed within a one-semester model. Students report many challenges in learning research methodology, including framing research questions, understanding the theory or literature, difficulties in performing data analysis, unfamiliarity with the technical language describing fundamental concepts, and lack of numeral knowledge to deal with quantitative methods.

2.2. Some Points

The difficulties of teaching research methods courses are challenging to address because there is inadequate pedagogical research on innovative ways of teaching the subject. That is why professors must not just teach students critical-thinking skills and give them opportunities to put them to use, but they must also *inspire* them to continue practicing those skills on their own across academic subjects and in all areas of life.

Given that thinking is something we do every waking hour and does not require practice fields, instruments, or special equipment, inspired students can apply the critical-thinking skills they learn in class to improve their grades and make better decisions in life, reinforcing their value and creating a virtuous cycle of continuous use.

2.3. Additional Implications

> **Students Thinking and Teaching Research Methods**
>
> The students' current level of understanding should be used as a base to build on when introducing new ideas.
>
> - The next level of thinking that follows the students' current understanding should be used to design graded sequences of activities that allow the students to move from their current understanding to the next higher level, constructing increasingly complex understandings.
> - It is helpful to introduce cognitive conflict, for example, by revealing shortcomings in the students' current ways of thinking because disequilibrium motivates students to construct new understandings (Griffin, 2004).

2.4. Creativity and Innovation

Creativity and innovation, while used interchangeably in many disciplines, are two different things. *Creativity* is defined as coming up with something original or unusual. Motivated by curiosity on top of a vast knowledge base, creativity allows one to shake up the normal way of thinking and come up with new solutions to a problem. *Innovation*, on the other hand, is creating something new that has obvious value to others. There is a very interesting space where both concepts can coexist and even complement each other: a *scientific research laboratory*. Being able to demonstrate science and research as a dynamic process often proves to be invaluable (Neutens and Rubinson, 2002).

Oftentimes, when *research is approached in the classroom, the static "core" is stressed, leaving little emphasis on the nature of applied research concepts* (Arnold, Gansneder, and Perrin, 2005).

2.5. Some Points

At first, this might sound ridiculous. Aren't the creative process and the scientific process entirely different? Isn't innovation reserved for industry and product development? In fact, scientific research is a field where there are no rules, no standards, and no direct expectations of an outcome. Fundamental research is meant to discover the unknown and solve problems that don't yet have solutions. It often doesn't go as planned and leads to solutions and problems not part of the original question. The nature of a material's science discipline is creative in itself, acknowledging the fact that problems, such as self-healing polymers and energy storage, cannot be solved with any one strict science discipline alone. These complex problems require complex solutions from scientists who can creatively combine their multiple fields of knowledge (Enago Academy, 2021).

2.6. Six Tips toward Increasing Scientific Creativity

- Knowledge is the basis for which creativity and innovation can develop. Make sure you are open to learning new things at all stages of the problem-solving process since new information might be the key to finding a creative solution.
- Take a break from the problem statement and let your mind wander. Research shows, by giving your mind time to focus on something else or to relax, you free your mind to come up with a newly innovative idea. In 1869, struggling to organize the chemical elements, Dmitri Mendeleev took a nap at his desk. While he slept, his subconscious mind kept working. In a dream, he "saw a table where all the elements fell into place as required," and this was the basis of our current periodic table.

- Open your mind. Perceptions and judgments can limit the information you take in. Don't let these feelings close your mind to a potentially creative idea.
- Rewrite the problem in a completely different way. You might see the solution from this perspective. Or ask a friend for help. Another pair of eyes may be able to see the problem in a different light.
- Try things others are not trying and look where they are not looking. Sometimes the answer is a creative twist on what people have not tried. Don't be afraid to be the one to give it a shot.
- Don't be afraid to get it wrong. Research is the best avenue for taking risks because of the freedom you have to solve problems no one has solved before. Edison made several thousand attempts before he discovered the one that worked (Flynn, J. R., 1987; Kim, K. H., 2011).

2.7. Innovative Teaching Strategies in Research Methods

Creating innovative methods for facilitating research, the following presents strategies to assist the educator in this process.

2.8. Teaching Research Method Using a Student-Centered Approach? Critical Reflections on Practice

Student-Centered Approaches Using Interactive Learning Activities in Small Group Teaching; Five Changes to Practice:

- Shifting the balance of classroom power from teacher to student;
- Designing content as a means to building knowledge rather than a "knowledge end" in itself;
- Positioning the teacher as facilitator and contributor rather than director and source of knowledge;

- Shifting responsibility for learning from teacher to learner; and
- Promoting learning through effective assessment (Barraket, 2005).

2.9. Designing Patterns for Teacher and Learner Activities That Emphasize Knowledge Integration

Some Instructors' Experiences
<ul><li>Repeated group work helped students understand different perspectives and think more critically and reflectively about their assumptions and values in relation to doing research.</li><li>Students enjoyed getting to know one another and felt confident to express themselves in class as a result of feeling comfortable with one another.</li><li>The use of primary source material kept the subject matter interesting and relevant.</li><li>And formal presentation of content from the lecturer remained important (Froyd, J. E., 2007).</li></ul>

Voice of the Instructor
I am particularly concerned with learning environment and learning content. While recognizing that the nature of assessment is a central concern of student-centered educational design, the changes in teaching practice considered below were introduced after the fact with regard to design and promotion of the subject to the students involved. As such, significant deviations from originally planned assessment were not possible. While this somewhat constrains the analysis of learning outcomes achieved in the shift in educational design, it also reflects the real-world dynamics of adapting curricula in university contexts (Crouch, C. H. and Mazur, E., 2001).

Voice of the Instructor

The change to practice in seeking to develop a more student-centered approach in this subject, I focused specifically on the role and nature of small group activities. As Hativa (2000) has identified, student-centered instructional methods include discussion, group work, role-playing, experiential learning, problem-based learning, and case-method teaching. All these methods were utilized in various combinations throughout the semester.

Voice of Instructor of Research Methodology

I have taught research methodology to undergraduate students, postgraduates, academic staff, and corporate executives for over seventeen years but have noticed that students are getting less motivated to study research methodology. This observation led to the development of a research program on the pedagogy of research methodology, focused on the questions:

- Why are students less engaged in research methods classes?
- How can we provide students with meaningful learning experiences in research methods?
- Why do teachers of research methods approach the teaching of the subject differently?

Laying a Solid Foundation for Research

The groundwork for teaching research begins with the delivering of the "materials" needed to start the process. Often we have used the approach of house-building as a real-world analogy. Selection of an appropriate "site" to build is similar to deciding a topic to research. Delivering of the materials to the site is not unlike seeking out references and supporting literature relative to the topic. The following discusses a foundational approach (Hoidn, S. and Olbert-Bock, S., 2016).

Active Learning Approach: Collaborative Learning
Proposed change: Stimulate undergraduate student interest through active and collaborative learning through the redesign of a course to include participation in a research project. Outcome: Students make good/great gains in content knowledge, skill acquisition, and overall confidence and comfort for major concepts in the research methods course. Course design: This course was previously taught in a lecture format where the students read peer-reviewed journals to understand the major concepts of research methodology. The active, collaborative learning project is created to help students work in a team and become more familiar with the research methodology that requires active participation in a research project conducted throughout the academic semester and involved continual feedback from the instructors. Students were randomly assigned to a group of three or four and will be introduced to the research project orally in class and through written handouts during the first class meeting. Student groups initially chose a topic from an instructor-generated list of feasible research ideas (Campisi and Finn, 2011; Bonwell, C. C. and Eison, J. A., 1991).

<table>
<tr><td>Teaching Research Method Using a Student-Centered Approach</td></tr>
<tr><td>

Active learning approaches: Case-study teaching, problem-based learning, group work, role-play, and simulation

Proposed change: Build experiential common ground and shift toward a more student-centered approach to enhance students' experiential understanding of the complexities and creativity of conducting effective research.

Outcomes: The shift toward student-centeredness significantly will enhance students' learning through the use of interactive small group activities and a high level of discussion and interaction.

This example highlights the challenges in teaching research methods to a diverse cohort of students.

Course design: Small group activities include icebreakers, scenario exercises, role-plays, and critical reflections to foster high levels of dialogue. Authentic learning will be fostered by including guest lectures and focusing the curriculum on current affairs (Barraket, 2005).

</td></tr>
</table>

Some Instructions to Instructors' Practical Sessions

Generate New Ideas (Research Topics)

Main goal: Sharing of ideas and synthesizing an array of topics will help stimulate thought and discussion versus simply having a person decide in isolation or with only an advisor

Steps:

- Start a class by having students use index cards to write down ideas they have generated.
- Have students switch index cards with one another to either add content to the ideas or generate a new idea.
- At the conclusion of three rounds of trading index cards, have a student volunteer to write the topics on a white board, chalkboard, etc. This will help others appreciate and visualize all the ideas.
- The class should be facilitated in a room with computer and Internet) access for each student; numbers will vary.
- Explain to the students that the purpose of the lesson is to identify various research search engines based on topics of interest. The instructor/facilitator should take students through a working example to familiarize them with all aspects of a valid search.
- Based on a topic of interest, students should be able to demonstrate a favorable outcome, proficiency, by generating a list of five to ten peer-reviewed research citations.

SECTION 2

Chapter 3

Syllabus of Innovative Research Methods

3.1. Background

To be a competent researcher, it is necessary to not only acquire skills in the techniques, but also to have an understanding of the philosophical issues that underpin academic research. Traditionally, these are often not well understood. As a result, many research methodology courses are quite superficial, with the emphasis being placed on collecting and analyzing data. This is not really sufficient for the purposes of quality academic research (Hoidn, S. and Olbert-Bock, S., 2016).

However, some good and innovative work is being done in this field in various parts of the world. And many universities are changing the way they teach research methodology to help educate and develop young researchers. It is believed being aware of these approaches to teaching will provide helpful insights into the types of issues academics are coping with when teaching research methodology today in various parts of the world. This chapter suggests a syllabus that encourages students to think as researchers, think critically and conduct creative research. The chapter simplifies the research content that solves significant challenges in learning research methodology. The content provided by this chapter is based on substantial innovation and change in current educational practices. Learning must become more social, authentic, adapted to individual motivations and abilities, reflective, and strategic, to name just a few challenges. The purpose of design research is to enable such change by inspiring, testing, and refining innovative practice in the classroom.

Note: Most of materials of this section are derived from authors' experiences in teaching and supervising research at undergraduate and postgraduate levels.

3.2. Main Objectives of the Course

- To make thinking visible. This concerns the thinking of the teachers and the students. The teachers should model scientific thinking to help students understand how problems are solved, for example, by means of simulations and visualizations. The students should be prompted to report on their ideas, critique and analyze their progress, and reflect on the nature of science.
- To enable students to learn from others. When students learn from one another, they encounter a broad range of views that help them develop personal criteria for decisions and make their solutions comprehensible to others.
- To promote autonomy and lifelong learning by engaging students in complex projects in which they practice critiquing, comparing, revising, rethinking, and reviewing their ideas. This

helps them contrast solutions, test potential connections, and solve novel, complex problems.

- To promote students make good/great gains in content knowledge, skill acquisition, and overall confidence and comfort for major concepts in the research methods course.

3.3. Description of the Course

The course equips the students with the essential knowledge and skills to successfully plan and implement an independent extended research project. It enables the students to identify and develop research questions and design an appropriate research strategy. All sessions will be interactive and include open classes and small group discussions and group working. Sessions include presentations from academics who present and share their experiences of using different methods of data collection and analysis of research. The course introduces the students to critical thinking to prepare them for the innovative contents of research methodology.

3.4. Methods of Teaching Research Method Course

The method requires an active participation in the research project and involves continual feedback from the instructors. Teaching methods adopt the following approaches:

- Active learning
- Collaborative learning
- Case-study teaching
- Problem-based learning
- Group working
- Role-playing

- Simulation
- Learner-centered design
- Hands-on research
- Reflective skills

3.5. Outline of the Course

3.5.1. Session 1: Critical Thinking and Research Methodology

Aim: Acquire students with knowledge and skills of critical thinking

What is critical thinking?

Critical thinking is learning to think independently and to develop one's opinions supported by existing evidence. In learning scenarios that promote and foster problem-solving and critical-thinking skills, it is much more difficult for the student to simply adhere to the role of the passive student; rather, this type of learning prompts the student to assume the role of a self-reliant thinker and researcher (S., Handfield, T. & Restall, G. (2009),Willingham, D. T. (2007).

Research and Critical Thinking

However, attaining critical-thinking skills does not come without its challenges, as students must be able to manage a vast array of resources within a series of complex network systems. This is especially true when students are asked to write a research paper, which is one of the most common methods for teaching critical-thinking skills. Inherent within writing a research paper are various levels of reasoning, with each level becoming progressively more abstract, complex, and effortful. This promotes higher-order thinking skill and more critical thought in the form of synthesis-level thinking and builds upon the prior skill levels in a hierarchical fashion. However, when confronted with this seemingly daunting task, many college students shy away, presumably because they lack these skills and, therefore, need to be taught how to learn and apply them (Wolcott, S. K., 2002).

Thinking Tools

Thinking tools use technology to allow students to convey and exchange ideas, actively construct knowledge, solve problems, and create nonlinguistic representations of what they have learned. During a course of study, students modify these representations to show their growth in understanding over time. This process helps teachers gauge student understanding and also helps students direct their learning (Elder, L. and Paul, R., 2005).

Ask the students to answer the following questions and then introduce them to model answer:

What do you call a strong-minded person?

Answer: Determined, firm, resolute, resolved, purposeful, purposive, sure, self-disciplined, strong-willed, uncompromising, unyielding, unbending, unwavering, unswerving, unfaltering, unshakeable, inexorable, forceful, persistent, persevering, tenacious, dogged, stubborn, dedicated, committed, stalwart (Akhtar, A., 2019)

How would you describe a thinker? (Smith, R. and Killogre, W. D. S., 2017)

Answer: A thinker is just what it sounds like—a person who does a lot of thinking. You can use the noun thinker when you talk about a smart, scholarly person who's known for being an intellectual or to describe someone who contemplates every choice at great length.

How do you describe someone who thinks a lot?

Answer: The word you are looking for is *pensive*. The single word *philosopher* is also used, often in a somewhat sarcastic way, to refer to a contemplative person or someone who remains silent while others are in a lively or heated discussion:

"Your baby is so quiet—he just sits in his chair."

"Yes, he's a philosopher."

3.5.2. Session 2: Exercises of Critical Thinking

Critical Thinking

Exercise 1: What is critical thinking in your words?

Critical thinking means making reasoned judgments that are logical and well-thought-out. It is a way of thinking in which you don't simply accept all arguments and conclusions you are exposed to but rather have an attitude involving questioning such arguments and conclusions (Willingham, D. T., 2007).

Deep Thinking (Byers, W., 2014)

Exercise 2: How do I become a deeper thinker? Discuss the following points:

- If something doesn't make sense to you, look for ways to expand your knowledge so you understand it.

- If you want to be a deep thinker, you have to get in the habit of asking deep questions. Ask about everything. To be a more insightful thinker, ask why repeatedly!

Are deep thinkers intelligent? Discuss with the students the following points:

- One's ability to think deeply may not be directly related to their IQ.
- However, being a deep thinker definitely enhances one's approach to situations.
- The elements associated with thinking deeply may certainly nurture one's intelligence in different ways.

Why is deep thinking important? Discuss answering this question with students.

- Deep thinking helps us realize there is often more than one way of thinking.
- It further enables us to entertain ideas without necessarily having to accept them.
- By thinking deeply, we can create and entertain thoughts that are more meaningful and valuable. This, in turn, greatly influences how we behave.

How can you tell if someone is deep? Discuss these seven points with students. Here are seven commonalities deep souls tend to express when they are being purely themselves:

- Bravely independent. Deep souls are independent all the way around.
- Meaning seekers.
- Deep divers.

- Knowledge quarters.
- Learn by making.
- Intuitively sensitive.
- Crave authentic understanding.

Understanding the Meaning of Research

Exercise 3: What does it mean to think things through? (Earley, M. A., 2014)

To think about all the different parts or effects of something for a period, especially in an effort to understand or make a decision about it, I need time to think this through. We have thought through the matter and have come to a decision.

Brainstorming

Ask the students to give answer to this question: How do I become a student's researcher?

Then introduce the following points to students:

- Learn to think like a scientist.
- Look for questions, not subjects.
- Mentoring is as important as research.
- Reach out with confidence.
- Start your research with reading and keep on reading.
- Set specific goals for yourself and let your mentors know.
- Research takes time.
- Find a healthy balance.

3.5.3. Session 3: Understand the Meaning of Research

Use active, collaborative learning methods to help students work in a team and become more familiar with the concept.

Organize students into groups. Ask them to discuss the following definitions of research and develop their understanding of what research is.

What is research?

Many attempts have been made to reach a working definition of research. According to Pandey and Mishra (2015), research is a combination of "re" and "search," which indicates searching more and more. Krause (2020) provides a working definition of research writing as the process of utilizing evidence from journals, books, magazines, the Internet, and specialists to convince the readers about a specific subject. Research is also defined as "a process of inquiry and investigation; it is systematic, methodical and ethical; research can help solve practical problems and increase knowledge" (Neville, 2007).

Research is reported as a manner of thinking and exploring several fields of knowledge to understand the specific issue and develop and test theories with the aim of making progress and advancement in the profession (Kumar, 2016).

As stated by Bocar (2013), research is the process of data collection, analysis, interpretation, and testing the applicability of the findings. One can define research as a scientific and systematic search for pertinent information on a specific topic. In fact, research is an art of scientific investigation; some authors define the meaning of research as a careful investigation or inquiry, especially through search for new facts in any branch of knowledge (Earley, M. A., 2014).

Research is, thus, an original contribution to the existing stock of knowledge, making for its advancement. The systematic approach concerning generalization and the formulation of a theory is also research. As such, the term *research* refers to the systematic method. Some people consider research as a movement, a movement from the known to the unknown. It is actually a voyage of discovery. We all possess the vital instinct of curiosity; for when the unknown confronts us, we wonder, and our inquisitiveness makes us probe and attain full and fuller understanding of the unknown. This inquisitiveness is the mother of all knowledge and the method, which a person employs for obtaining the knowledge of whatever the unknown, can be termed as research (Creswell, J. W., 2009).

<table><tr><td>

Exercise

</td></tr><tr><td>

Research: A Way of Thinking. Discuss this paragraph.

Research is undertaken within most professions. More than a set of skills, research is a way of thinking: examining critically the various aspects of your day-to-day professional work; understanding and formulating guiding principles that govern a particular procedure; and developing and testing new theories for the enhancement of your practice. It is a habit of questioning what you do and a systematic examination of the observed information to find answers with a view to instituting appropriate changes for a more effective professional service (Bernarte, R., 2019).

</td></tr></table>

3.5.4. Session 4: Objectives and Types of Research

Objectives of Research

The purpose of research is to discover answers to questions through the application of scientific procedures. The main aim of the research is to find out the truth hidden and has not been discovered yet. Though each research study has its specific purpose, we may think of research objectives as falling into a number of following broad groupings (Della Porta, D. and Keating, M. eds., 2008; Punch, K. F., 2005):

- To gain familiarity with a phenomenon or to achieve new insights into it; studies with this object in view are termed as exploratory research studies
- To portray accurately the characteristics of a particular individual, situation, or group; studies with this object in view are known as descriptive research studies
- To determine the frequency with which something occurs or with which it is associated with something else; studies with this object in view are known as diagnostic research studies
- To test a hypothesis of a causal relationship between variables; such studies are known as hypothesis-testing research studies

Types of Research

The basic types of research are as follows:

Descriptive versus Analytical. Descriptive research includes surveys and fact-finding inquiries of different kinds. The major purpose of descriptive research is to describe the state of affairs as it exists at present. In social science and business research researchers quite often use Research Methodology: An Introduction 3 the term Ex post facto research for descriptive research studies. The main characteristic of this method is the researcher has no control over the variables; he can only report what has happened or what is happening. Most ex post facto research projects are used for descriptive studies in which the researcher seeks to measure such items as, for example, frequency of shopping, preferences of people, or similar data. Ex post facto studies also include attempts by researchers to discover causes even when they cannot control the variables. The methods of research utilized in descriptive research are survey methods of all kinds, including comparative and correlation methods. In analytical research, on the other hand, the researcher has to use facts or information already available and analyze these to make a critical evaluation of the material.

Applied versus Fundamental. Research can either be applied (action) research or fundamental (basic or pure) research. Applied research aims at finding a solution for an immediate problem facing a society or an industrial/business organization, whereas fundamental research is mainly concerned with generalizations and with the formulation of a theory. "Gathering knowledge for knowledge's sake is termed 'pure' or 'basic' research. Research concerning some natural phenomenon or relating to pure mathematics are examples of fundamental research (Kumar, R., 2011).

3.5.5. Session 5: Development of New Ideas of Research

Help Students' Thinking

- The students' current level of understanding should be used as a base to build on when introducing new ideas.
- The next level of thinking that follows the students' current understanding should be used to design graded sequences of activities that allow the students to move from their current understanding to the next higher level, constructing increasingly complex understandings.
- It is helpful to introduce cognitive conflict, for example, by revealing shortcomings in students' current ways of thinking

because disequilibrium motivates students to construct new understandings (Toledo-Pereyra, L. H., 2011).

Development of the Ideas

With the help of the following four routes of constructing ideas, ask the students to select suitable route for developing new ideas.

Linn (2006) distinguishes among four major routes students often follow as they construct and modify their set of ideas:

First, some students tend to conceptualize. They start with a broad range of ideas but quickly focus on normative ideas. They often neglect the sources of their original views and readily embrace abstract principles from instructional materials.

Second, some students tend to experiment. They test and change their numerous ideas in different contexts, adding normative and nonnormative ideas to explain observations and make sense of everyday experiences. These students pay attention to intriguing contexts.

Third, some students strategize. They separate the school context from other contexts and seek to succeed with minimal effort, often relying on rote learning and trying to figure out ways to answer questions likely to be on the test.

Fourth, there are students who contextualize ideas—that is, they view all ideas in isolated specific contexts instead of seeking connections. This limits their explanations, for example, when they try to argue that two aspects of one principle are separate (e.g., heating and cooling).

Students should be able to better reconcile their ideas and to develop criteria to sort out ideas so they can build coherent accounts of scientific phenomena (Linn et al., 2006).

Generate New Ideas (Research Topics)

Main Goal: Sharing of ideas and synthesizing an array of topics will help to stimulate thought and discussion versus simply having a person decide in isolation or with only an advisor

Steps

- Start a class by having students use index cards to write down idea have been generated,
- Have students switch the index cards with each other to either add content to the ideas, or generate a new idea
- At the conclusion of three rounds of trading index cards, have a student volunteer to write the topics on a white board, chalkboard, etc.
- This will help others to appreciate and visualize all of the ideas.
- The class should be facilitated in a room with computer (internet) access for each student (numbers will vary).
- Explain to the students that the purpose of the lesson is to identify various research search engines based on topics of interest. The instructor/facilitator should take students through a working example so as to familiarize them with all aspects of a valid search. • Based on a topic of interest, students should be able to demonstrate a favorable outcome (proficiency) by generating a list of 5 to 10 peer reviewed research citations Linn (2006

3.5.6. Session 6: Concepts and Variables

What is concept? A concept is a thought or idea. If you're redecorating your bedroom, you might want to start with a concept, such as *flower garden* or *outer space*. It's a general idea about a thing or group of things derived from specific instances or occurrences.

What is a concept in a research study? Formally and logically developed ideas about classes of phenomena a researcher seeks to study, the *building blocks* of theory.

These can take many different forms but should all be tied together with an underlying logic or framework for them to not only make sense on their own, but also mean something when taken as part of a whole; or put another way, they need consistency (Morin, J. F., 2012).

What is variable? A variable is a quantity that may change within the context of a mathematical problem or experiment. Typically, we use a single letter to represent a variable. The letters x, y, and z are common generic symbols used for variables. A variable is a special type of amount or quantity with an unknown value. The opposite of a variable—that is, a known value—is called a constant (Bevans, R., 2019).

How Concepts, Variables, and Attributes Are Related to One Another

Concept stands for an understanding drawn from a particular fact or logic. A concept could also be an established procedure. Variables are indicators or measure of the concept. Attributes are categories of the variable.

Knowingly or unknowingly, we use different kinds of concepts in our everyday conversations. Some of these concepts have been developed over time through our shared language. Sometimes we borrow concepts from other disciplines or languages to explain a phenomenon of interest. For instance, the idea of *gravitation* borrowed from physics can be used in business to describe why people tend to *gravitate* to their preferred shopping destinations. Likewise, the concept of *distance* can be used to explain the degree of social separation between two otherwise collocated individuals. Sometimes we create our concepts to describe a unique characteristic not described in prior research (Burns N, Grove S. (2007 and Kaur, S. P. (2013).

Concepts may also have progressive levels of abstraction. Some concepts, such as a person's *weight* are precise and objective, while other concepts, such as a person's *personality* may be more abstract and difficult to visualize. A *construct* is an abstract concept specifically chosen or *created* to explain a given phenomenon. A construct may be a simple concept, such as a person's *weight*, or a combination of a set of related concepts, such as a person's *communication skill*, which may consist of several underlying concepts, such as the person's *vocabulary*, *syntax*, and *spelling*. The former instance, weight, is a *one-dimensional construct*, while the latter, communication skill, is a *multidimensional construct*, i.e., it consists of multiple underlying concepts. The distinction between constructs and concepts are clearer in multidimensional constructs, where the higher order abstraction is called a construct and the lower order abstractions are called concepts. However, this distinction tends to blur in the case of one-dimensional constructs (Nebeker, C. at el., (2015).

Scientific research requires *operational definitions* that define constructs in terms of how they will be empirically measured. For instance, the operational definition of a construct such as *temperature* must specify whether we plan to measure temperature in Celsius, Fahrenheit, or Kelvin scale. A construct such as *income* should be defined in terms of whether we are interested in monthly or annual income, before-tax or after-tax income, and personal or family income. One can imagine that constructs such as *learning*, *personality*, and *intelligence* can be quite hard to define operationally.

Depending on their intended use, variables may be classified as independent, dependent, moderating, mediating, or control variables. Variables that explain other variables are called *independent variables*, those that are explained by other variables are *dependent variables*, those that are explained by independent variables while also explaining dependent variables are *mediating variables* or intermediate variables, and those that influence the relationship between independent and dependent variables are called *moderating variables*. As an example, if we state that higher intelligence causes improved learning among students, then intelligence is an independent variable and learning is a dependent variable. There may be other extraneous variables not pertinent to explaining a given dependent variable but may have some impact on the dependent variable. These variables must be controlled for in a scientific study and are, therefore, called *control variables* (Polit, D.F. and Beck, C.T. (2014), Ellström, P.-E., Elg, M. et al., (2020).

3.6. Sessions of the Research Process

3.6.1. Session 1: Steps of Research

These sessions describe methods for planning and conducting scientific research, from formulation of problems to setting research objectives, to designing the study, including methods of data collection, statistical analysis, as well as interpretation and dissemination of the results. Research is an academic activity, and as such, the term should be used in a technical sense. According to Clifford Woody, research comprises defining and redefining problems, formulating hypothesis, or suggesting solutions; collecting, organizing, and evaluating data; making deductions and reaching conclusions; and last, carefully testing the conclusions to determine whether they fit the formulating hypothesis (Morin, F., 2012).

One should remember the various steps involved in a research process are not mutually exclusive, nor they are separate and distinct. They do not necessarily follow one another in any specific order, and the researcher has to be constantly anticipating at each step in the research process the requirements of the subsequent steps. However, the following order concerning various steps provides a useful procedural guideline regarding the research process:

Various Steps of Research Process
(1) Formulating the research problem
(2) Extensive literature survey
(3) Developing the hypothesis
(4) Preparing the research design
(5) Determining sample design
(6) Collecting the data
(7) Executing the project
(8) Analyzing of data
(9) Hypothesis-testing
(10) Generalizing and interpreting
(11) Preparing the report or presenting the results, i.e., formal writeup of conclusions reached

3.6.2. Session 2: Formulating the Research Problem and Objectives

In writing research, one of the most important parts that constitute a great troublesome for EFL, in general, is defining the research problem. More specifically, some researchers find it difficult to determine the exact problem to be addressed in the research, making them fail to fulfill the objectives of the study. Ifeoma (2019) argues that undergraduate and postgraduate students encounter difficulty in identifying the problem of research. A broad problem is featured as unclear and vague, so narrowing down the problem help identifying and addressing that problem and, in turn, designing good research questions (Boudah, 2011). When writing a research problem, three main elements need to be taken into consideration: First, the general overview of the focus topic to be investigated in the study. Second, explanation and justification of the problem: presenting logical reasons for the significance of addressing the problem, which can be attained through providing evidence from literature, recommending further research to be implemented or drawn from the researcher's experience. Third, the research gap shows how the current study is different from previous studies within the research field. The research gap reveals the problem has not been examined by past literature, and the current study attempts to bridge that gap (Bryman, 2007). This marks the beginning of a research study and is the most difficult and important step. This involves identifying and stating the problem in specific terms.

To achieve this, you review the literature related to the problem to know what other researchers have done and discovered and to identify the possible methodology for conducting the research.

Conceptualizing the Problem:

- Identifying the problem (What is the problem?)
- Prioritizing the problem (Why is this an important problem?)
- Rationalizing the problem (Can the problem be solved, and what are the benefits to society if the problem is solved?)

Writing the Statement of the Problem

Background

- Literature review (What do we already know?)
- Formulating the objectives
- Framing the questions according to general and specific objectives
- Developing a testable hypothesis to achieve the objectives

Settlement of the Objectives

The statement of the objective is of basic importance because it determines the data which are to be collected, the characteristics of the data which are relevant, relations which are to be explored, the choice of techniques to be used in these explorations, and the form of the final report. If there are certain pertinent terms, the same should be clearly defined along with the task of formulating the problem. In fact, formulation of the problem often follows a sequential pattern, where a number of formulations are set up, each formulation more specific than the preceding one, each one phrased in more analytical terms, and each more realistic in terms of the available data and resources.

How to Develop and Write Good Research Aims and Objectives

Good, clear statements indicating a project's research aims, objectives, or questions do not normally spring forth fully formed in a sudden eureka moment. They tend to emerge slowly, after considerable thought, and take time to develop and finalize. When first designing a project, try to give yourself plenty of time to think through your aims and objectives. Ideally, this thinking should not be done in a hurry or under pressure. Read around your subject. Analyze previous studies in the area. Look at how other researchers frame their aims and objectives. What key technical terms or concepts do they employ? The better you understand the published literature on your topic, the more likely you are to be able to effectively conceptualize your research aims and objectives (Evensen, D. H. and Hmelo, C. E., 2000).

Linking Research Objectives to Research Methods

Having a clear understanding of a project's research objectives or questions paves the way for other important decisions about the design and running of the project. This includes decisions about which populations or demographic groups to include in the study and what data collection methods to use. In some poorly designed studies, the research methods chosen for the study do not properly match the research objectives. As a result, the data obtained often does not directly address the research objectives. Think carefully about the relationship between your research objectives or questions and your choice of research methods. Aim to describe as clearly as possible how the sampling, data-gathering, and analysis methods you intend to use will help meet each of the research objectives or questions (Hancké, B., 2009).

Exercises for Developing Research Objectives

1. Develop a suitable research aim and three specific objectives for a research topic in which you have an interest.
2. Change the research objectives you developed above into research questions.
3. Using personal contacts or an Internet search, find some examples of completed research proposals on a topic you are interested. Note the style used to write the research aims and objectives.

Research Questions

In some situations, rather than stating research objectives, researchers will prefer to use an alternative to research objectives, where the key issues to be focused on in a research project are stated in the form of questions.

A *research question* is *a question that a research project sets out to answer.* [1] Choosing a research question is an essential element of quantities and qualitative research. Investigation will require data collection and analysis, and the methodology for this will vary widely. Good research questions seek to improve knowledge on an important topic and are usually narrow and specific.

To form a research question, one must determine what type of study will be conducted, such as a qualitative, quantitative, or mixed study. Additional factors, such as project funding, may not only affect the research question itself but also when and how it is formed during the *research* process. Literature suggests several variations on criteria selection for constructing a research question (Mattick, K.; Johnston, J.; De la Croix, A., 2018).

3.6.3. Session 3: Extensive Literature Survey

Once the problem is formulated, a brief summary of it should be written down. At this juncture, the researcher should undertake extensive literature survey connected with the problem. For this purpose, the abstracting and indexing journals and published or unpublished bibliographies are the first place to go to. Academic journals, conference proceedings, government reports, books, etc., must be tapped, depending on the nature of the problem. In this process, it should be remembered one source will lead to another. The earlier studies, if any, similar to the study at hand should be carefully studied. A good library will be a great help to the researcher at this stage (Della Porta, D. and Keating, M., eds., 2008).

3.6.4. Session 4: Development of Working Hypotheses

After extensive literature survey, researcher should state in clear terms the working hypothesis or hypotheses. Working hypotheses are tentative assumptions made to draw out and test their logical or empirical consequences. As such, the manner in which research hypotheses are developed is particularly important since they provide the focal point for research. They also affect the manner in which tests must be conducted in the analysis of data and, indirectly, the quality of data required for the analysis. In most types of research, the development of working hypotheses plays an important role. Hypotheses should be very specific and limited to the piece of research at hand because they have to be tested. The role of the hypotheses is to guide the researcher by delimiting the area of research and to keep them on the right track. It sharpens their thinking and focuses their attention on the more important facets of the problem. It also indicates the type of data required and the type of methods of data analysis to be used.

How does one go about developing working hypotheses? The answer is by using the following approach:

(a) Discussions with colleagues and experts about the problem, its origin, and the objectives in seeking a solution

(b) Examination of data and records, if available, concerning the problem for possible trends, peculiarities, and other clues

(c) Review of similar studies in the area or of the studies on similar problems

(d) Exploratory personal investigation that involves original field interviews on a limited scale with interested parties and individuals with a view to secure greater insight into the practical aspects of the problem

Thus, working hypotheses arise as a result of a priori thinking about the subject, examination of the available data and material, including related studies, and the counsel of experts and interested parties. Working hypotheses are more useful when stated in precise and clearly defined terms. It may as well be remembered, occasionally, we may encounter a problem where we do not need working research methodology hypotheses, especially in the case of exploratory or formulative research, which does not aim at testing the hypothesis. But as a general rule, specification of working hypotheses is another basic step of the research process in most research problems Casula, M.; Rangarajan, N., and Shields, P. (2021).

3.6.5. Session 5: Preparing the Research Design

The research problem having been formulated in clear cut terms, the researcher will be required to prepare a research design, i.e., they will have to state the conceptual structure within which the research would be conducted. The preparation of such a design facilitates research to be as efficient as possible, yielding maximum information. In other words, the function of research design is to provide for the collection of relevant evidence with minimal expenditure of effort, time, and money. But how all these can be achieved depends mainly on the research purpose. Research purposes may be grouped into four categories: exploration, description, diagnosis, and experimentation.

A flexible research design, which provides opportunity for considering many different aspects of a problem, is considered appropriate if the purpose of the research study is that of exploration. But when the purpose happens to be an accurate description of a situation or of an association between variables, the suitable design will be one that minimizes bias and maximizes the reliability of the data collected and analyzed. There are several research designs, such as experimental and nonexperimental hypothesis-testing. Experimental designs can be either informal designs, such as before and after without control, after only with control, before and after with control; or formal designs, such as completely randomized design, randomized block design, Latin square design, simple and complex factorial designs; out of which the researcher must select one for their project. The preparation of the research design appropriate for a particular research problem involves usually the consideration of the following: the means of obtaining the information; the availability and skills of the researcher and his staff, if any; explanation of the way in which selected means of obtaining information will be organized and the reasoning leading to the selection; the time available for research; and the cost factor relating to research, i.e., the finance available for the purpose (Krause, S., 2020; Kumar, R., 2016; Moses, J. W. and Knutsen, T. L., 2007; and Hancké, B., 2009).

3.6.6 Session 6: Determining Sample Design

All the items under consideration in any field of inquiry constitute a "universe" or "population." A complete enumeration of all the items in the "population" is known as a census inquiry. It can be presumed in such an inquiry, when all the items are covered, no element of chance is left, and highest accuracy is obtained. But in practice, this may not be true. Even the slightest element of bias in such an inquiry will get larger and larger as the number of observations increases. Moreover, there is no way of checking the element of bias or its extent, except through a resurvey or use of sample checks. Besides, this type of inquiry involves a great deal of time, money, and energy. Not only this, but also census inquiry is not possible in practice under many circumstances. For instance, blood testing is done only on sample basis. Hence, quite often we select only a few items from the universe for our study purposes. The items so selected constitute what is technically called a sample. The researcher must decide the way of selecting a sample or what is popularly known as the sample design. In other words, a sample design is a definite plan determined before any data are actually collected for obtaining a sample from a given population. Samples can be either probability samples or non-probability samples. With probability samples, each element has a known probability of being included in the sample, but the non-probability samples do not allow the researcher to determine this probability. Probability samples are those based on simple random sampling, systematic sampling, stratified sampling, cluster/area sampling; whereas non-probability samples are those based on convenience sampling, judgment sampling, and quota sampling techniques. A brief mention of the important sample designs is as follows:

Deliberate sampling is also known as purposive or non-probability sampling. This sampling method involves purposive or deliberate selection of particular units of the universe for constituting a sample that represents the universe. When population elements are selected for inclusion in the sample based on the ease of access, it can be called convenience sampling. If a researcher wishes to secure data from, say, gasoline buyers, he may select a fixed number of petrol stations and may conduct interviews at these stations. This would be an example of convenience sample of gasoline buyers. At times such a procedure may give very biased results, particularly when the population is not homogeneous. On the other hand, in judgment sampling, the researcher's judgment is used for selecting items he considers as representative of the population. For example, a judgment sample of college students might be taken to secure reactions to a new method of teaching. Judgment sampling is used quite frequently in qualitative research, where the desire happens to be to develop hypotheses rather than to generalize to larger populations.

Simple random sampling is also known as chance sampling or probability sampling, where each and every item in the population has an equal chance of inclusion in the sample, and each one of the possible samples, in case of finite universe, has the same probability of being selected. For example, if we have to select a sample of three hundred items from a universe of fifteen thousand items, then we can put the names or numbers of all the fifteen thousand items on slips of paper and conduct a lottery. Using the random number tables is another method of random sampling. To select the sample, each item is assigned a number from one to fifteen thousand. Then three hundred five-digit random numbers are selected from the table. To do this, we select some random starting point, and then a systematic pattern is used in proceeding through the table. We might start in the fourth row, second column, and proceed down the column to the bottom of the table and then move to the top of the next column to the right. When a number exceeds the limit of the numbers in the frame, in our case over fifteen thousand, it is simply passed over and the next number selected that does fall within the relevant range. Since the numbers were placed in the table in a completely random fashion, the resulting sample is random. This procedure gives each item an equal probability of being selected. In case of infinite population, the selection of each item in a random sample is controlled by the same probability, and that successive selections are independent of one another.

Systematic sampling—in some instances, the most practical way of sampling is to select every fifteenth name on a list, every tenth house on one side of a street, and so on. Sampling of this type is known as systematic sampling. An element of randomness is usually introduced into this kind of sampling by using random numbers to pick up the unit with which to start. This procedure is useful when sampling frame is available in the form of a list. In such a design, the selection process starts by picking some random point in the list, and then every nth element is selected until the desired number is secured.

Stratified sampling—if the population from which a sample is to be drawn does not constitute a homogeneous group, then stratified sampling technique is applied to obtain a representative sample. In this technique, the population is stratified into a number of nonoverlapping subpopulations or strata, and sample items are selected from each stratum. If the items selected from each stratum is based on simple random sampling the entire procedure, first stratification and then simple random sampling is known as stratified random sampling.

Quota sampling—in stratified sampling, the cost of taking random samples from individual strata is often so expensive that interviewers are simply given quota to be filled from different strata, the actual selection of items for sample being left to the interviewer's judgment. This is called quota sampling. The size of the quota for each stratum is generally proportionate to the size of that stratum in the population. Quota sampling is, thus, an important form of non-probability sampling. Quota samples generally happen to be judgment samples rather than random samples.

Cluster sampling and *area sampling*—cluster sampling involves grouping the population and then selecting the groups or the clusters rather than individual elements for inclusion in the sample. Suppose some department store wishes to sample its credit card holders. It has issued its cards to fifteen thousand customers. The sample size is to be kept, say, 450. For cluster sampling, this list of fifteen thousand card holders could be formed into one hundred clusters of 150 card holders each. Three clusters might then be selected for the sample randomly. The sample size must often be larger than the simple random sample to ensure the same level of accuracy because cluster sampling procedural potential for order bias and other sources of error is usually accentuated. The clustering approach can, however, make the sampling procedure relatively easier and increase the efficiency of field work, especially in the case of personal interviews. Area sampling is quite close to cluster sampling and is often talked about when the total geographical area of interest happens to be a big one. Under area sampling, we first divide the total area into a number of smaller nonoverlapping areas, generally called geographical clusters, then a number of these smaller areas are randomly selected, and all units in these small areas are included in the sample. Area sampling is especially helpful, where we do not have the list of the population concerned. It also makes the field interviewing more efficient since the interviewer can do many interviews at each location.

Multistage sampling is a further development of the idea of cluster sampling. This technique is meant for big inquiries, extending to a considerably large geographical area like an entire country. Under multistage sampling, the first stage may be to select large primary sampling units, such as states, then districts, then towns, and finally certain families within towns. If the technique of random sampling is applied at all stages, the sampling procedure is described as multistage random sampling.

Sequential sampling is somewhat a complex sample design, where the ultimate size of the sample is not fixed in advance but is determined according to mathematical decisions on the basis of information yielded as the survey progresses. This design is usually adopted under acceptance sampling plan in the context of statistical quality control. In practice, several of the methods of sampling described above may well be used in the same study; in which case, it can be called mixed sampling. (McCombes, S., 2019; Hinkel, E., ed., 2011; Lavrakas, P. J., 2008).

3.6.7. Session 7: Collecting Data

In dealing with any real-life problem, it is often found data at hand are inadequate, and hence, it becomes necessary to collect appropriate data. There are several ways of collecting appropriate data, which differ considerably in context of money costs, time, and other resources at the disposal of the researcher. Primary data can be collected either through experiment or through survey. If the researcher conducts an experiment, he observes some quantitative measurements or the data; with the help of which, he examines the truth contained in his hypothesis. But in the case of a survey, data can be collected by any one or more of the following ways:

(i)   Observation: This method implies the collection of information by way of investigator's observation, without interviewing the respondents. The information obtained relates to what is currently happening and is not complicated by either the past behavior or future intentions or attitudes of respondents. This method is, no doubt, an expensive method, and the information provided by this method is also very limited. As such, this method is not suitable in inquiries where large samples are concerned.

(ii) Personal interview: The investigator follows a rigid procedure and seeks answers to a set of preconceived questions through personal interviews. This method of collecting data is usually carried out in a structured way, where output depends upon the ability of the interviewer to a large extent.

(iii) Telephone interviews: This method of collecting information involves contacting the respondents on telephone. This is not a very widely used method, but it plays an important role in industrial surveys in developed regions, particularly when the survey has to be accomplished in a very limited time.

(iv) Mailing of questionnaires: The researcher and the respondents do come in contact with each other if this method of survey is adopted. Questionnaires are mailed to the respondents with a request to return after completing the same. It is the most extensively used method in various economic and business surveys. Before applying this method, usually, a pilot study for testing the questionnaire is conducted, which reveals the weaknesses, if any, of the questionnaire. The questionnaire to be used must be prepared very carefully so it may prove to be effective in collecting the relevant information.

(v) Schedules: Under this method, the enumerators are appointed and given training. They are provided with schedules containing relevant questions. These enumerators go to respondents with these schedules. Data are collected by filling up the schedules by enumerators on the basis of replies given by respondents. Much depends upon the capability of enumerators so far as this method is concerned. Some occasional field checks on the work of the enumerators may ensure sincere work.

The researcher should select one of these methods of collecting the data, taking into consideration the nature of investigation, objective and scope of the inquiry, financial resources, available time, and the desired degree of accuracy. Though he should pay attention to all these factors, much depends upon the ability and experience of the researcher.

3.6.8. Session. 8. Execution of the project: Execution of the project is a very important step in the research process. If the execution of the project proceeds on correct lines, the data to be collected would be adequate and dependable. The researcher should see the project is executed in a systematic manner and in time. If the survey is to be conducted by means of structured questionnaires, data can be readily machine-processed. In such a situation, questions as well as the possible answers may be coded. If the data are to be collected through interviewers, arrangements should be made for proper selection and training of the interviewers. The training may be given with the help of instruction manuals, which clearly explain the job of the interviewers at each step. Occasional field checks should be made to ensure the interviewers are sincerely and efficiently doing their assigned job. A careful watch should be kept for unanticipated factors to keep the survey realistic as much as possible. This, in other words, means steps should be taken to ensure the survey is under statistical control so the collected information is in accordance with the predefined standard of accuracy. If some of the respondents do not cooperate, some suitable methods should be designed to tackle this problem. One method of dealing with the nonresponse problem is to make a list of the nonrespondents and take a small sub-sample of them, and then with the help of experts, vigorous efforts can be made for securing response (Hinkel, E., ed., 2011; Bhandari, P. 2019; Barab, S., 2006).

3.6.8. Session8: Analysis of Data

After the data have been collected, the researcher turns to the task of analyzing them. The analysis of data requires a number of closely related operations, such as establishment of categories, the application of these categories to raw data through coding, tabulation, and then drawing statistical inferences. The unwieldy data should necessarily be condensed into a few manageable groups and tables for further analysis. Thus, the researcher should classify the raw data into some purposeful and usable categories. Coding operation is usually done at this stage, through which the categories of data are transformed into symbols that may be tabulated and counted. Editing is the procedure that improves the quality of the data for coding. With coding, the stage is ready for tabulation. Tabulation is a part of the technical procedure, wherein the classified data are put in the form of tables. The mechanical devices can be made use of at this juncture. A great deal of data, especially in large inquiries, is tabulated by computers. Computers not only save time but also make it possible to study large number of variables, affecting a problem simultaneously. Analysis work after tabulation is generally based on the computation of various percentages, coefficients, etc., by applying various well-defined statistical formulae. In the process of analysis, relationships, or differences supporting or conflicting with original or new hypotheses should be subjected to tests of significance to determine with what validity data can be said to indicate any conclusion(s). For instance, if there are two samples of weekly wages, each sample being drawn from factories in different parts of the same city, giving two different mean values, then our problem may be whether the two mean values are significantly different or the difference is just a matter of chance. Through the use of statistical tests, we can establish whether such a difference is a real one or is the result of random fluctuations. Similarly, the technique of analysis of variance can help us in analyzing whether three or more varieties of seeds grown on certain fields yield significantly different results or not. In brief, the researcher can analyze the collected data with the help of various statistical measures (*Judd, C. and Mc Cleland, G. (1989)*;Sherman, R. (2014)& Field, J. (2009).

3.6.9. Session 9: Hypothesis-Testing

After analyzing the data as stated above, the researcher is in a position to test the hypotheses, if any, he had formulated earlier. Do the facts support the hypotheses, or they happen to be contrary? This is the usual question that should be answered while testing hypotheses. Various tests, such as Chi square test, t-test, F-test, have been developed by statisticians for the purpose. The hypotheses may be tested through the use of one or more of such tests, depending upon the nature and object of research inquiry. Hypothesis-testing will result in either accepting the hypothesis or in rejecting it. If the researcher had no hypotheses to start with, generalizations established on the basis of data may be stated as hypotheses to be tested by subsequent researches in times to come (Rice, J. A., 2007 and Bellhouse, P., 2001).

3.6.10. Session 10: Generalizations and Interpretation

If a hypothesis is tested and upheld several times, it may be possible for the researcher to arrive at a generalization, i.e., to build a theory. As a matter of fact, the real value of research lies in its ability to arrive at certain generalizations. If the researcher had no hypothesis to start with, he might seek to explain his findings on the basis of some theory. It is known as interpretation. The process of interpretation may quite often trigger off new questions, which, in turn, may lead to further researches (Hubbard, R. and Bayarri, M. J., 2013).

3.6.11. Session 11: Preparation of the Report or the Thesis

Finally, the researcher has to prepare the report of what has been done by him. Writing of the report must be done with great care, keeping in view the following:

1. The layout of the report should be as follows: (i) the preliminary pages, (ii) the main text, and (iii) the end matter.

In its preliminary pages, the report should carry title and date, followed by acknowledgments and foreword. Then there should be a table of contents, followed by a list of tables and list of graphs and charts, if any, given in the report. The main text of the report should have the following parts: (a) Introduction: It should contain a clear statement of the objective of the research and an explanation of the methodology adopted in accomplishing the research. The scope of the study, along with various limitations, should as well be stated in this part. (b) Summary of findings: After introduction, there would appear a statement of findings and recommendations in nontechnical language. If the findings are extensive, they should be summarized. (c) Main report: The main body of the report should be presented in logical sequence and broken down into readily identifiable sections. (d) Conclusion: Toward the end of the main text, the researcher should again put down the results of his research clearly and precisely. In fact, it is the final summing up. At the end of the report, appendices should be listed in respect of all technical data. Bibliography, i.e., list of books, journals, reports, etc., consulted, should also be given in the end. Index should also be given, especially in a published research report. Research methodology report should be written in a concise and objective style in simple language, avoiding vague expressions, such as "it seems," "there may be," and the like.

3. Charts and illustrations in the main report should be used only if they present the information more clearly and forcibly.

4. Calculated "confidence limits" must be mentioned, and the various constraints experienced in conducting research operations may as well be stated. Criteria of good research, whatever may be the type of research, works and studies, one thing that is important is they all meet on the common ground of scientific method employed by them. One expects scientific research to satisfy the following criteria:

1. The purpose of the research should be clearly defined and common concepts be used.
2. The research procedure used should be described in sufficient detail to permit another researcher to repeat the research for further advancement, keeping the continuity of what has already been attained.
3. The procedural design of the research should be carefully planned to yield results that are as objective as possible.
4. The researcher should report with complete frankness flaws in procedural design and estimate their effects upon the findings.
5. The analysis of data should be sufficiently adequate to reveal its significance, and the methods of analysis used should be appropriate. The validity and reliability of the data should be carefully checked.
6. Conclusions should be confined to those justified by the data of the research and limited to those for which the data provide an adequate basis.
7. Greater confidence in research is warranted if the researcher is experienced, has a good reputation in research, and is a person of integrity.

3.7. Sessions, Exercises to Encourage Students Thinking of Research Process

Bereiter, C. and M. Scardamalia (2008), Evensen, D. H., & Hmelo, C. E. (2000). Barab, S. (2006), Burns, Grove Susan.K 2007 Kara,H. (2012). Reddy,C.(2016)

3.7.1. Exercise 1: What is a good research?

Ask the students to answer the question then discuss the following points:

- Does the research have a solid hypothesis?
- Is there evidence of a *comprehensive literature review* from reputable sources that clearly defines a target area for valuable research?
- Is the research team allocating sufficient time/resources to do the job properly, or were compromises made to accommodate the available funding?
- Is there evidence of a willingness to refine the hypothesis and research strategy if needed?
- Are the expectations of the implications of the research realistic?

3.7.2. Exercise 2: Skills to Develop Critical Thinking, Think as Researchers

What is analysis?

Analyzing means carefully examining information to understand, interpret, and explain it. This can involve identifying assumptions, gaps, and connections between such things as data, reasoning, or evidence.

A thorough analysis prepares you well for a final evaluation, where you form judgments and draw conclusions.

In the identifying stage, you will have asked critical questions to determine what kind of information you are working with, who produced the information, and for whom. Analyzing involves thinking very carefully about this information and the claims being made.

This involves looking beyond the surface of what is said and examining assumptions and reasoning behind a perspective.

Discuss with the Students: The Building Blocks of Analysis

The building blocks of analysis are questions. Questioning scrutinizes your sources of information and the arguments being presented; for example:

- *Why* did the author write this text? Or *why* was this data produced? Is there any evidence of bias?
- *Why* did the author make particular assumptions and not others?
- *Why* was certain evidence presented?
- *How* does or doesn't the evidence provided support the conclusions reached?
- *Who* would benefit from this proposal or argument, and is there evidence of a conflict of interest?
- *What* information has been omitted from this source, and *why*?

When asking critical questions, you demonstrate you can think carefully about the evidence that supports your arguments and the arguments of others. *Each point of analysis communicates your thinking toward a final evaluation, judgment, or conclusion.*

3.7.3. Exercise 3: What is an argument?

The common understanding of an *argument* typically involves an emotional and volatile state, where people yell and hurl personal insults. At university, arguments mean something different.

An argument is a structured set of reasons or objections that seek to support or refute a central claim. The central claim is called a *contention, conclusion, hypothesis,* or *position*—this is what the arguer/author wants you to believe. *Claims* given in support of other claims are called *reasons. Claims* that refute other claims are called *objections* or *rebuttals.*

Discuss with Students: Analyzing Arguments

Ask analytical questions for a deep understanding of the reasoning that constitutes an argument, for example:

- Does the argument contain assumptions? What are they?
- Is the reasoning balanced? Are different perspectives taken into account?
- What is the background to this issue? Are there any implicit arguments?
- Is the argument *logical*?
- Are the claims adequately supported by evidence?

Discuss with Students: How do I evaluate arguments?

Recall *arguments* are contentions with supporting reasons. Arguments aim to support or challenge contentions, drawing on evidence to do so.

To determine whether an argument is reasonable, you could ask a few evaluative questions:

- Is the contention clearly stated? Does it make sense?
- Is reliable evidence provided for each reason?
- Do the reasons and evidence provided fully support the contention—that is, is there a logical connection between the reasons and the conclusion?
- Are any objections to the contention clearly and convincingly rebutted or refuted with evidence and logic?
- Is there evidence of any *logical fallacies* in the argument?

We are always making these judgments based on the information available at the time. If more information becomes available, a good critical thinker will be willing to reevaluate their judgment based on this new evidence.

In general, when we say that a statement or belief is true, we're saying it is supported by facts or a large body of evidence. Thus, when someone says we're living in "post-truth" times, they're saying people no longer base their beliefs or statements on facts or objective evidence.

3.7.4. Exercise 4: Argument = Contention + Reason(s)

Discuss the following example:

Contention: All university students should receive free public transport.

Reason: It would assist them financially.

Argument: All university students should receive free public transport because it would assist them financially.

This example illustrates the basic argument formulation of contention + reason. Note that the argument uses the term *because* to link these two claims.

Arguments are everywhere, but of course, that doesn't mean we should accept them!

3.7.5. Exercise 5: Inductive Arguments

Inductive arguments provide a likelihood or probability that if the premises are true, then the conclusion is true. The likelihood or probability is considered *strong or weak*, unlike deductively valid arguments, where there is a guarantee of truth. Inductive arguments typically arise where a generalization or an analogy is provided, building on a small number of observations to a generalized conclusion about a given category or class. (Refer below to see how the *scientific method* uses observations and experiments).

A claim resulting from samples, observations, case studies, or examples can lead to a generalized statement or statistical inference about a whole population.

Example:

The percentage of the university student sample satisfied with the catering at their orientation program is 75%. Therefore, 75% of the university student population were satisfied with the catering at their orientation program. Note: The inference made about the population is based on the sample group and may not be accurate.

Scientific and everyday reasoning employ *induction*, drawing general conclusions from specific observations. For example, a person's opinion that cramming for a test increases performance may be based on her memory of passing an exam after pulling an all-night study session. Similarly, a researcher's conclusion *against* cramming might be based on studies comparing the test performances of people who studied the material in different ways, e.g., cramming versus study sessions spaced out over time. In these scenarios, scientific and everyday conclusions are drawn from a limited *sample* of potential observations. The process of induction alone does not seem suitable enough to provide trustworthy information, given the contradictory results. What should a student who wants to perform well on exams do? One source of information encourages her to cram, while another suggests spacing out her studying time is the best strategy. To make the best decision with the information at hand, we need to appreciate the differences between personal opinions and scientific statements, which requires an understanding of science and the nature of scientific reasoning.

Exercise 6: Test Yourself: Inductive or Deductive?

A. The stove was on, and the water in the pot was boiling over. The front door was standing open. These clues suggest the homeowner left unexpectedly and in a hurry.

B. Gravity is associated with mass. Because the moon has a smaller mass than the Earth, it should have weaker gravity.

C. Students don't like to pay for high-priced textbooks. It is likely many students in the class will opt not to purchase a book.

D. To earn a college degree, students need one hundred credits. Janine has eighty-five credits, so she cannot graduate.

3.8. Writing a Research Proposal

A research proposal is a very specific genre of writing. The purpose of a research proposal is (a) to persuade your reader of the value of your research question, (b) to show you have a clear idea of where your research sits in existing knowledge, and (c) to demonstrate how you plan to answer your question. Therefore, your research proposal needs to answer three basic questions: What is your research problem? Why is it important? And how do you propose to solve it?

What is your research problem?

The research problem is the heart of the research proposal and the most intellectually complex part of the proposal. Therefore, it will require the most work. A helpful way to start is to separate out the component parts of the research problem: What are your research objectives? What do you want to learn by conducting this research project? And what questions will get you there?

What are your research objectives?

Your research objectives will determine your research question, so take some time to figure out what you want to find out through your research.

Research Questions

Our research objectives will determine our research questions, but we also have to be careful about how we formulate our research questions. As we're likely to be drawn to research topics about which we feel strongly, there is a risk that our research questions are not questions but rather statements of what we currently believe to be right.

The Role of Literature in Your Research Proposal

The role of a literature review in a research project is often misunderstood. It is *not* where you describe everything you have read in relation to your topic. The function of a literature review is to demonstrate the value of your research project by analyzing prior research and identifying an area in which further research can be fruitfully conducted by you. Research proposals are generally short, usually no longer than two to five pages. Therefore, you need to think about ways to demonstrate your knowledge and understanding of the field succinctly.

How will you conduct your research?

No matter how interesting or urgent your question puzzle, only viable research proposals will be successful. Therefore, you must address how you propose to conduct your research project by clearly demonstrating how you will progress from inception to completion. There are two things you need to think about in your proposal: What is your methodology? And what resources are available to you?

Methodology

Once you have a research question clear, the next step is to outline your data and methods. What data will you examine to answer your questions? Will you be using preexisting data or generating new data? How will you go about collecting it? Have you checked if it is possible to access the data you wish to use? Are there any ethical issues you need to consider? Are you sure this data will actually be able to answer the research questions you have set yourself? And if not, do you need to revise your research question or the data you are using? The creation of a research proposal is not linear—you will inevitably go back and forth the research problem, the research literature, and your methodology. You can ensure the value and coherency of your research proposal by being open to how your research puzzle and methodology will shape and inform one another.

Resources

In writing your research proposal, you need to make a realistic and pragmatic assessment of the resources you have at your disposal to conduct a piece of original research and tailor your objectives, questions, and methods accordingly. What you can achieve in a final year undergraduate thesis is very different from what you can achieve in a doctoral degree. There is no point writing a research proposal that requires you to interview individuals if you have no funds to travel to meet them. Likewise, there is no point in proposing research that requires you to interview people you have no way contacting. Similarly, you will be creating a lot of difficulty for yourself if you need to learn three new languages to conduct those interviews. Therefore, think about what you can reasonably achieve in light of the time, money, and skills you already possess. That is not to say you should not try to acquire new skills to conduct new research, but you should be able to point to the time and money you have to enable you to acquire them. If space allows, it is a good idea to include a research timeline in your proposal to demonstrate you have given thought to how you will complete your project.

Final Thoughts

It should now be clear that writing a research proposal requires a lot of preparation. Once you have done the hard work of figuring out the what, why, and how of your proposal, the next task will be to translate that into a well-written proposal. Here, you will face the challenge of limited space. Therefore, you should endeavor to be direct and succinct in your writing. Work with drafts and discuss your ideas with others. This will help you figure out what you really want to say. The clearer you are on the elements above, the easier writing will be.

4. References

Zhang, J. Q. (2009) Critical Reflection and Student Autonomy. Retrieved from Course Hero. https://www.coursehero.com/file/p2jb4hb/paper-by-Researcher-Jane-Qinjuan-Zhang-titled-Critical-Reflection-and-Student/.

Drew, P.; Chatwin, J.; and Collins, S. (2001) Conversation analysis: a method for research into interactions between patients and health-care professionals, Department of Sociology, University of York, York, YO10 5 DD, UK, Blackwell Science Ltd 2001 Health Expectations, 4, pp. 58±70.

Griffin, S. (2004) "Contributions of central conceptual structure theory to education," in Demetriou, A. and A. Raftopoulos (eds.), Cognitive Developmental Change. Theories, Models and Measurement, Cambridge University Press, Cambridge, UK, pp. 264–295.

Neutens, J. J. and Robinson, L. (2002) Research techniques for the health sciences. Benjamin Cummings, San Francisco.

Facione, P. (2007) Critical thinking: What it is and why it counts. Millbrae, CA: Insight Assessment, California Academic Press. American Philosophical Association, Critical Thinking: A Statement of Expert Consensus for Purposes of Educational Assessment and Instruction."

Facione, P. A. (2000). The disposition toward critical thinking: Its character, measurement, and relation to critical-thinking skill. *Informal Logic, 20*(1), 61–84.

Fischer, S. C.; Spiker, V. A.; and Riedel, S. L. (2009) *Critical thinking training for army officers, volume 2: A model of critical thinking.* (Technical Report). Arlington, VA: U.S. Army Research Institute for the Behavioral and Social Sciences.

Halpern, D. F. (2001) Assessing the effectiveness of critical thinking instruction. *The Journal of General Education, 50*(4), 270–286.

Ku, K. Y. (2009) Assessing students' critical-thinking performance: Urging for measurements using multi-response format. *Thinking Skills and Creativity, 4*(2009), 70–76.

McPeck, J. E. (1990) Critical thinking and subject specificity: A reply to Ennis. *Educational Researcher, 19*(4), 10–12.

Pithers, R. T., and Soden, R. (2000) Critical thinking in education: A review. *Educational Research, 42*(3), 237–249.

Thayer-Bacon, B. J. (2000) *Transforming critical thinking: Thinking constructively.* New York, NY: Teachers College Press.

Casula, M.; Rangarajan, N., and Shields, P. (2021) The potential of working hypotheses for deductive exploratory research, Vol.:(0123456789) Quality & Quantity (2021) 55:1703–1725 https://doi.org/10.1007/s11135-020-01072-9

Tim van Gelder (2005) Teaching Critical Thinking: Some Lessons From Cognitive Science, College Teaching, 53:1, 41-48, DOI: 10.3200/CTCH.53.1.41-48.

Froyd, J. E. (2007) Evidence for the efficacy of student-active learning pedagogies. *Project.*

Earley, M. A. (2014) A Synthesis of the Literature on Research Methods Education. Teaching in Higher Education, *19*(3), 242–253.

Enago Academy. (2021) The Importance of Critical-Thinking Skills in Research.

Campisi, J. and Finn, K. E. (2011) Does Active Learning Improve Students' Knowledge of and Attitudes toward Research Methods? *Journal of College Science Teaching, 40*(4), 38–45.

Butchart, S.; Handfield, T.; and Restall, G. (2009) Using Peer Instruction to Teach Philosophy, Logic, and Critical Thinking. Teaching Philosophy, *32*(1), 1–40, DOI: 10.5840/teachphil20093212, https://www.researchgate.net/publication/242686933

Willingham, D. T. (2007) Critical thinking: Why is it so hard to teach? *American Educator,* 31,8-19.http://www.aft.org/sites/default/files/periodicals/Crit_Thinking.pdf

Barraket, J. (2005) Teaching Research Method Using a Student-Centered Approach? Critical Reflections on Practice. Journal of University Teaching and Learning Practice, *2*(2), 3. Available at:http://ro.uow.edu.au/jutlp/vol2/iss2/3

Burns N, Grove S. (2007) Understanding nursing research: Building an evidence-based practice. 4. St. Louis, MO: Elsevier; pp. 60–96.

Kaur, S. P. (2013). Variables in research. Indian Journal of Research and Reports in Medical Sciences, 3(4), 36-38.

O'Hare, L. O., and McGuinness, C. (2009) Measuring critical thinking, intelligence, and academic performance in psychology undergraduates. *The Irish Journal of Psychology, 30*(3–4), 123–131.

Gellin, A. (2003) The effect of undergraduate student involvement on critical thinking: A meta-analysis of the literature 1991–2000. *Journal of College Student Development, 44*(6), 746–762.

Creswell, J. W. (2009) *Research Design: Qualitative, Quantitative, and Mixed Method Approaches* (3rd ed). Thousand Oaks, CA: Sage. (See Chapter 7).

Krølner, R.; Due, P.; Rasmussen, M.; Damsgaard, M. T.; Holstein, B. E.; Klepp, K. I.; et al. (2009) Does school environment affect 11-year-olds' fruit and vegetable intake in Denmark? *Social Science & Medicine, 68* (8), 1416–1424.

Lewin, S. and Green, J. (2009). Ritual and the organization of care in primary care clinics in Cape Town, South Africa. *Social Science & Medicine, 68* (8), 1464–1471.

Liebert, R. and Gavey, N. (2009) "There are always two sides to these things": Managing the dilemma of serious adverse effects from SSRIs. *Social Science & Medicine, 68* (10), 1882–1891.

Miller, F. A.; Sanders, C. B.; and Lehoux, P. (2009). Imagining value, imagining users: Academic technology transfer for health innovation. *Social Science & Medicine, 68* (8), 1481–1488.

Punch, K. F. (2005) Introduction to Social Research: Quantitative and Qualitative Approaches (2nd ed). London: Sage. (See Chapter 3).

Della Porta, D. and Keating, M., eds. (2008) *Approaches and Methodologies in the Social Sciences: A Pluralist Perspective*, Cambridge: Cambridge University Press.

Mattick, K.; Johnston, J.; and De la Croix, A. (2018) "How to . . . Write a good research question." The Clinical Teacher. 15 (2): 104 108. doi:10.1111/ tct.12776. PMID 29575667. S2CID 4360924.

Hancké, B. (2009) *Intelligent Research Design: A Guide for Beginning Researchers in Social Sciences,* Oxford, Oxford University Press.

Moses, J. W. and Knutsen, T. L. (2007) *Ways of knowing: Competing Methodologies and Methods in Social and Political Research,* Basingstoke, Palgrave Macmillan.

Schostak, J. and Schostak, J. F. (2013) *Writing Research Critically: Developing the Power to Make a Difference*, Routledge.

Casula, M; Nandhini, R.; Shields, P. M. (October 2021). "The potential of working hypotheses for deductive exploratory research." *Quality & Quantity.* 55 (5): 1703–1725. doi:10.1007/s11135-020-01072-9. PMC 7722257. PMID 33311812.

Krause, S. (2020) The process of research writing. Libre Text. Retrieved from https://bit.ly/3leGajC.

Kumar, R. (2016) Research methodology: A step-by-step guide for beginners. Sage Publications.

De Sanchez, M. A. Using critical-thinking principles as a guide to college-level instruction. *Teach Psychol.* 1995;22:72–74. [Google Scholar]

Dingfelder, S. F. With red pen in hand. *gradPSYCH.* 2005;3:28–29. [Google Scholar]

Lawson, T. J. Assessing psychological critical thinking as a learning outcome for psychology majors. *Teach Psychol.* 1999;26:207–209. [Google Scholar]

Newell, K. M. Kinesiology: Challenges of Multiple Agendas. *Quest.* 2007;59:5–24. [Google Scholar]

Yanchar, S. C. and Slife, B. D. Teaching critical thinking by examining assumptions. *Teach Psychol.* 2004;31:85–90. [Google Scholar]

Zablotsky, D. Why do I have to learn this if I'm not going to graduate school? Teaching research methods in a social psychology of aging course. *Educ Gerontol.* 2001;27:609–622. [Google Scholar]

Polit, D. F. and Beck, C. T. Nursing Research, Principles and Methods. 7 edition. Philadelphia: Lippincott Williams & Wilkins; 2004. pp. 29–32, 37–38.

Ahmed, F. and Mahboob, U. (2016) Analysis of Research Proposals and Challenges Faced by Postgraduate Trainees in Internal Medicine and Allied Disciplines during Fellowship Training Program: A Qualitative Study. *Khyber Medical University Journal, 8*(2).

Almutairi, N. H. (2007) The influence of educational and sociocultural factors on the learning styles and strategies of female students in Saudi Arabia (Doctoral dissertation, University of Leicester)

Al-Qaseri, I. (2016) How to Write a Research Paper: Exploring the challenges faced by Yemeni undergraduate students in writing their graduation research projects. LAP Lambert Academic Publishing, German.

Ankawi, A. (2015) The academic writing challenges faced by Saudi students studying in New Zealand. Thesis submitted to Auckland University of Technology as MA requirement.

Kikula, I. S. and Quorro, M. A. S. (2007). Common Mistakes and Problems in Research Proposal Writing. Dar es Salaam: Research on Poverty Alleviation (REPOA).

Kothari, C. R. (2004) *Research methodology: Methods and techniques.* New Age International.

Tayie, S. (2005) *Research methods and writing research proposals.* Pathways to Higher Education.

Kilburn, D.; Nind, M.; and Wiles, R. (2014). Learning as Researchers and Teachers: The Development of a Pedagogical Culture for Social Science Research Methods? British Journal of Educational Studies, *62*(2), 191–207.

Lewthwaite, S. and Nind, M. (2016). Teaching Research Methods in the Social Sciences: Expert Perspectives on Pedagogy and Practice. *British Journal of Educational Studies, 64*(4), 413–430.

Christopher S. Main L. Felipe Perrone Greg L. Schrock.(2014). DATA VISUALIZATION FOR NETWORK SIMULATIONS, Proceedings of the 2014 Winter Simulation Conference, At: Savannah, GA, DOI: 10.1109/WSC.2014.7020149

Paul J Silivia (2012) Curiosity and Motivation The Oxford Handbook of Human Motivation Edited by Richard M Ryan DOI 10.1093 oxford 9780195399820.013 0010 University of North Carolina at Greensboro

Bambrick-Santoyo, P. (2010). Driven by Data: A Practical Guide to Improve Instruction The Main Idea .current education books summarizes, Published by Jossy-Bass.

Walker, S. E. (2003) Active Learning Strategies to Promote Critical Thinking, Journal of Athletic Training 2003;38(3):263–267 q by the National Athletic Trainers' Association, Inc. www.journalofathletictraining.org.

Fung, D. (2017) A connected curriculum for higher education. London, UCL press. Retrieved from http://www.ucl.ac.uk/ucl-press/browse-books/a-connected-curriculum-for-higher-education.

Campisi, J. and Finn, K. E. (2011) Does Active Learning Improve Students' Knowledge of and Attitudes toward Research Methods? *Journal of College Science Teaching, 40*(4), 38–45.

Barr, R. and Tagg, J. (1995) From Teaching to Learning: A New Paradigm for Undergraduate Education. *Change, 27*(6), 12–25.

Barraket, J. (2005) Teaching Research Method Using a Student-Centered Approach? Critical Reflections on Practice. Journal of University Teaching and Learning Practice, *2*(2), 3.

Barron, K. E. and Apple, K. J. (2014). Debating Curricular Strategies for Teaching Statistics and Research Methods: What Does the Current Evidence Suggest? Teaching of Psychology, *41*(3), 187–194.

Biggs, J. (1999) Teaching for Quality Learning at University, Buckingham: Open University Press.

Crouch, C. H. and Mazur, E. (2001) Peer instruction: Ten years of experience and results. *American Journal of Physics, 69*(9), 970–977.

Bonwell, C. C. and Eison, J. A. (1991) Active learning; Creating excitement in the classroom. Retrieved from http://www.ydae.purdue.edu/lct/hbcu/documents/active_learning_creating_excitement_in_the_classroom.pdf.

Hoidn, S. and Olbert-Bock, S. (2016) Learning and Teaching Research Methods in Management Education: Development of a Curriculum to

Combine Theory and Practice—A Swiss Case. *International Journal of Educational Management, 30*(1), 43–62.

Kilburn, D.; Nind, M.; and Wiles, R. (2014) Learning as Researchers and Teachers: The Development of a Pedagogical Culture for Social Science Research Methods? British Journal of Educational Studies, *62*(2), 191–207.

Wolcott, S. K. (2002) Critical thought on critical thinking research Journal of Accounting Education Volume 20, Issue 2, Spring 2002, pp. 85–103.

Elder, L. and Paul, R. (2005) Critical Thinking: Tools for Taking Charge of Your Professional and Personal Life The Foundation for Critical Thinking.

Bernarte, R. (2019). Research a Way of Thinking. Research Methodology.

Ryan Smith and William D. S. Killgore (2014) Deep Thinking, https://doi.org/10.1142/9789814618045_0005, p.p.98-124,William Byers(Concordia University, Canda).

Byer, W. (2014) Deep Thinking What Mathematics Can Teach Us About the Mind, (Concordia University, Canada) https://doi.org/10.1142/9247 | November 2014,World Scientific, Pages: 264

Kumar, R. (2011) Research Methodology: A Step-by-Step Guide for Beginners. 3rd Edition. Sage, New Delhi.

Nebeker, C.; Simon, G.; Kalichman, M.; Talavera, A.; Booen, E.; and Lopez-Arenas, A. (2015) Building Research Integrity and Capacity

(BRIC): An Interactive Guide for Promotores/Community Health Workers. San Diego, CA: BRIC Academy.

Ellström, P. E.; Elg, M.; Wallo, A.; Berglund, M.; and Kock, H. () Interactive research: concepts, contributions and challenges Journal of Manufacturing Technology Management ISSN: 1741-038X.

Morin, J. F.; Olsson, C.; and Atikan, E. Ö. (2012) Research Methods in the Social Sciences: An A-Z of key concepts Edited by Oxford University Press.

Evensen, D. H., and Hmelo, C. E. (2000) *Problem-based learning: A research perspective on learning interactions.* Mahwah, NJ: Lawrence Erlbaum.

Sherman, R. (4 November 2014) Business intelligence guidebook: From data integration to analytics. Amsterdam. ISBN 978-0-12-411528-6. OCLC 894555128.

Field, J. (2009) "Dividing listening into its components," Listening in the Language Classroom, Cambridge: Cambridge University Press, pp. 96–109, doi:10.1017/cbo9780511575945.008, ISBN 978-0-511-57594-5, retrieved May 29, 2021.

Judd, C. and McCleland, G. (1989) Data Analysis. Harcourt Brace Jovanovich. ISBN 0-15-516765-0.

Rice, J. A. (2007) Mathematical Statistics and Data Analysis (3rd ed.). Thomson Brooks/Cole.

Bellhouse, P. (2001) "John Arbuthnot," in Statisticians of the Centuries by C. C. Heyde and E. Seneta, Springer, pp. 39–42, *ISBN 978-0-387-95329-8.*

Hubbard, R. and Bayarri, M. J. (2013) *P Values are not Error Probabilities Archived September 4, 2013, at the Wayback Machine*. A working paper that explains the difference between Fisher's evidential *p*-value and the Neyman–Pears.

Bevans, R. (2020) Types of Variable | Definitions and Easy Examples, Published on November 21, 2019 . Revised on March 2, 2021.

Walsh, M. and Wigens, L. (2003) Introduction to Research. Cheltenham: Nelson Thornes.

Hinkel, E., ed. (2011) *Handbook of research in second language teaching and learning* (Vol. 2). Routledge.

Hyland, F. (2013) Understanding the Challenges Faced by EFL Postgraduate Writers and Their Self-initiated Writing Strategies. In *Symposium on Second Language Writing*.

McCombes, S. (2019) Sampling Methods | Types and Techniques Explained.

Lavrakas, P. (2008), Sample Management in Encyclopedia of Survey Research Methods Chapter, DOI:https://dx.doi.org/10.4135/9781412963947

Bhandari, P. (2019) Data Collection | A Step-by-Step Guide with Methods and Examples Schriber.

Kara, H. (2012) *Research and Evaluation for Busy Practitioners: A Time-Saving Guide*. Retrieved from https://en.wikipedia.org/wiki/Research.

Kaur, S. P. (2013) Variables in research, Review Article IJRRMS 2013;3(4), IJRRMS | VOL-3 | No.4 | OCT - DEC | 2013, pp:36–38.

Alleva, E. (2019) *What is Research?* Retrieved from https://www.hampshire.edu/dof/what-is-research.

Polit, Denise F.& Beck, CT. (2004) . Nursing Research: Principles and Methods. 7 edition. Pliladephia, Publisher: Lippincott Williams & Wilkins, Philadelphia,2004; 2004. p 29-32,37-38.

Kerlinger Fred N. Foundation of Behavioral Research. 2nd edition. U.S.A: Holt, Rinehart and Winston, Inc; 1983. p 29-40. rd 3. Burns, Grove Susan.K. Understanding Nursing Research. 4 edition. Missouri: Elsevier Publication; 2007. p 125-129.

Kerlinger, Fred N. *Foundations of Behavioral Research.* (2nd ed.) New York: Holt, Rinehart and Winston,

Bereiter, C. and Scardamalia, M. (2008) "Toward Research-based Innovation," in *Innovating to Learn, Learning to Innovate,* OECD, Paris, pp. 67–88.

Reddy,C. (2016) *Why research is important?.* Retrieved from https://content.wisestep.com/research-important-students-humans-education.

De Bono, E. (2005) *De zes denkende hoofddeksels* [*Six Thinking Hats*] (16th ed.). Amsterdam: Uitgeverij.

Lamm, A. J. (2015) Integrating Critical Thinking into Extension Programming #1: Critical Thinking Defined. University of Florida. http://www.edis.ifas.ufl.edu/.